3

Postcards from Poland by Joseph Kuhn Carey
Chicago Poetry Press, Chicago, Illinois 60622
Copyright © 2013, 2014 by Joseph Kuhn Carey
ChicagoPoetry.com | ChicagoPoetryPress.com | PoetryAward.org
All rights reserved
Printed in the United States of America

Cover Photography: Joseph, Renata, Joey and Nicholas Carey, Danuta Plussa, Mark Plussa
Back Cover Artwork: Nicholas Carey
Cover and interior formatting: CJ Laity
Photo of Mr. Carey: Renata Carey
Postcard and postmark/stamp images used through Fair Use

"Sizzling Fiddlers Sling" finished in 18th place (out of 50 selected poems) in the 7th Annual Writer's Digest Poetry Awards Contest and was published in the 7th Annual Writer's Digest Poetry Competition Collection in 2012. "Sizzling Fiddlers Sling" was also selected in the 2012 Highland Park Poetry "Poetry That Moves" Contest (and subsequently appeared on the inside display areas of public buses running between the cities of Evanston and Highland Park, Illinois, as well as within the city of Waukegan, Illinois, for the entire month of April, 2013). "Sitting in a Swing" was published in the 2013 Journal of Modern Poetry/JOMP 15 poetry collection. "Nine Holes Near Krakow" was selected in the 2013 Highland Park Poetry/Poetry Challenge Contest and published in an HPP Contest Winners Booklet & on the HPP website. All of the rest of the poems in "Postcards From Poland" are published here for the first time.

Special Delivery

From the moment I stepped onto the curved, rugged, beautifully-worn cobblestones of Krakow's massive main square in the summer of 2011 during a memorable and inspiring two-and-a-half-week trip to the Polish cities of Krakow and Zakopane with my wife and sons, as well as my mother-in-law and brother-in-law, I felt at home, almost as if the surrounding sights and sounds were whispering to me and all I had to do was listen closely to hear the magical murmuring river of Poland's gorgeous, luminescent mind, heart, story and song. There was something mystical and moving in the people, buildings, landscape, churches and faith that filled me with so many wonderful and unforgettable images, I knew I had to start capturing things in words, to try and make three-dimensional inner snapshots that could be bottled up and sent back home, like imaginary postcards, which could each paint an immediate, colorful picture of a country and place, letting the recipient feel the excitement and share in the same adventure my eyes, mind, body and spirit were on.

Everyone has received a postcard at some point. They're the winged messengers of exploration, relaxation, restoration and the in-motion travel "experience." So small and yet so powerful, packing a wallop on both sides with a colorful picture that can startle or baffle or make you laugh, accompanied by a brief description and a dashed-off-but-exciting series of lines that usually contain unbridled gusto, delight, wonder and joy. For a moment, you're "one" with the person who sent the postcard, sharing in the dance of a distant or foreign culture, custom or place, bonded for a few seconds hundreds or thousands of miles apart. You can try, but you can't help wishing you really were there, whisked away from your own hum-drum everyday existence to the razzle-dazzle, light and pop of another location, suddenly dropped like a tuxedoed Cary Grant into the middle of a dashing, exciting Hollywood action adventure movie scene.

Another deep, resonating reason for our trip was to take my Poland-born mother-in-law back to her homeland with her two adult children, to reconnect with a country and people and create indelible new memories. She hadn't traveled to Poland together with her two children in several decades and this would be the chance of a lifetime, as well as a wonderful experience for our own sons to share in this magical family moment.

The route to America (and Chicago) for my mother-in-law had been an arduous one since being pulled from her home in Skalat (in the southeastern part of Poland) on April 13, 1940 during World War II as a five-year-old in the dark of night and forced by soldiers from the NKVD (the Soviet Secret Police) onto a crowded, rattling, freezing train cattle-car with her mother and two younger sisters for five or six horrific weeks before arriving in the remote, frigid, desolate village of Simipolka in Kazakhstan (Russia), where they would all live with several other frightened, fatherless Polish families in the simple, humble back rooms of a Russian family's house. Surrounded by countless deep feet of snow through which the passageways seemed like endless curving white tunnels and terrified of the packs of hungry wolves that roamed through the village at night and would often put their paws up on the windows of the little homes to look inside, she lived in these harsh circumstances for several years as a displaced person without a country, followed by (after Joseph Stalin's grant of "amnesty") several more years in Polish refugee camps in Uzbekistan, Iran (Persia), Lebanon and England. As if this wasn't a bleak-enough existence for a young child, she also experienced the heart-wrenching loss of her mother and sisters during this time due to malnutrition & illness caused by this grim, grinding, endless journey. Fortunately, her father, a Polish educator who had been arrested by the NKVD in January of 1940 and deported to a northern Siberian labor camp, survived. After his

6

"amnesty" release, he joined the newly formed Polish Army and fought against WWII foes while tracking down his sole surviving daughter through numerous refugee camps and orphanages by letter, word-of-mouth, friends, and acquaintances before finally, and joyfully, locating her in an orphanage hospital in Isfahan, Iran (Persia). Seventy-one years after being ruthlessly snatched from her beloved birthplace and country, she, too, was going home again to Poland with her children and grandchildren, as a quiet, true, humble and grateful survivor, which made the trip all the more meaningful for everyone.

During our stay in Krakow, we lived in a rustic, three-bedroom apartment (one reportedly used at one time as an office and sleeping quarters by famed World War I Polish war hero, statesman and leader Józef Piłsudski) and, due to the fact that three family members in our group spoke fluent Polish, we were able to interact with the locals in meaningful, dynamic ways during each eventful, unscheduled, full-of-surprises day, and blend in with the populace as much as possible. Each morning in Krakow, we'd improvise a new plan after a simple tea and toast breakfast around a long wooden table in our apartment and wander out into the streets, passing gorgeous churches, wonderful old mortar-cracked mysterious townhouses and elegant Old World buildings that featured ornate swirling wrought-iron balconies and tall double-entry doors, following the cobblestones and sidewalks toward the center of the town, later branching off to explore the nooks and crannies on side-streets before re-gathering for buoyant outdoor lunches or dinners, and, finally, searching (like sweet-tooth detectives on the prowl) for another delightful ice-cream shop on the way home for dessert. Sometimes, we'd journey outside the city to explore and see additional intriguing villages & towns and sights, sometimes we'd hop on a boat in the river and float up and down to let time stand still and hover in the moment, just absorbing the visual feast around us on either river bank. Other times, we'd simply ride the electric trolley-cars that snaked around the town, the horse-drawn carriages that clip-clopped merrily through the streets, or the busy, crowded local buses.

In the beautiful Tatra Mountain-base town of Zakopane, we made another "home" in a simple two-bedroom apartment in a quaint little bed and breakfast villa filled with gorgeous carved wood decorations inside and outside. Each day was jam-packed with new natural wonders reached by cable-car, funicular railway, bus, taxi or horse-drawn wagon and each night overflowed with the amazing fiddle-featuring folk music quartets in all of the restaurants along hilly, vibrant Krupówki Street. By dim-lit candlelight, the sturdy, rough-hewn wooden restaurant tables glowed and the air was filled with crackling music and sudden, strong vocal bursts from the energetic, colorfully-dressed young musicians, who would often also stamp their feet and clap their hands during songs, as they proudly carried on a long-time mountain folk tradition. The entire town seemed to be made of beautifully carved wood, each house more decoratively astonishing than the last, all roads seemingly leading down across the river to the wooden-stall marketplace full of furs, toys, wood-carvings, hats, walking sticks and oscypek, a mysterious salty smoked round cheese made from sheep's milk, as well as the shiny blue-and-yellow rail line cars leading up to the stunning scenic views on top of Gubałówka Hill.

Without a doubt, it was an unforgettable & magical trip and I hope you'll find the following poems that resulted from this journey as entertaining, enjoyable and enchanting to read as they were to write!

Sto lat!

Joseph Kuhn Carey
Glencoe, Illinois

For Renata, Joey and Nicholas,

my precious trio of world-traveling partners

Luggage Lost

Luggage lost
somewhere between
Chicago, Warsaw and Krakow,
all of the essential things
gone, jettisoned into space,
whirling in the travel jet-stream,
landing who knows where,
negotiations flow with the
domestic baggage desk, Polish words rattling
back and forth between the counter
and our little group,
before a phone call is finally made,
to the international side of the
airport and, low and behold,
the bags have been found and the
trip can begin again!

First Night

First night in Krakow,
strolling the huge public squares,
the street-lamps lit like
sweet sacred candles,
astonished at the beauty
of the ancient city and its
magnificent sprawl,
each cobblestone so
curved, worn and rugged
as if time had been secretly stolen
and stored in the odd shapes and cracks below,
straight ahead, the breath-taking, stage-lit
Sukiennice market hall
rises like a palace in an oasis of dreams,

arched, forever long and full of history
that it will tell to only
a select few who wander
inside and look, pausing
for a moment to ponder
the past, present and future,
a butterfly's wings, a glint of light
as a laughing child runs past,
or even a pigeon flock's zany zig-zag landing path,
all of the things that catch
a tired traveler's just-opening
hungry evening eyes.

Inside the Big Bronze Head

Inside the big bronze head
sitting sadly on its side in the main
Krakow Cloth Hall square, you feel
strange, like you're within
the fabled Trojan Horse,
waiting until nightfall
to emerge and strike,
but then you peer out through
the big bronze eye slits,
nose and mouth,

& you can't help but smile
because you're inside
someone else's head,
drumming on the metal
innards with your hands
and feet, lost in the dark
recesses, happy at last
to crawl out to daylight
and let the next set of
mind travelers in for
the moving-grooving show.

A Cart Full of Matches

A wooden cart full of matches
in cardboard boxes of all
shapes, sorts and sizes
sits quietly on a side street,
as if waiting for time to turn back
a century or more
to the days of horse-drawn carriages
and muddy streets and
men in tall black boots smoking
hand-rolled cigarettes,

a woman stands next to the cart,
dressed in an old-time peasant
dress, a colorful scarf wrapped
around her head,
the matches are wooden and thick,
ready for striking,
like little torpedoes packed away
in forgotten gray sheds,
the peeling paint on the cart
appears ancient, faint,
indecipherable,
a beautiful mystery
to behold beside
the woman's soft Mona Lisa smile.

The Lamps

The wrought-iron lamps
of Krakow hang
curved, quiet, still,
full of history and
burnished knowledge
about all those who
pass below on the
worn cobblestones,
hurrying to destinations
in all directions as
if the world might end

at any second, caught
up in clocks and time
while the lamps watch
all and know no master,
just the constant wearing
of the wind and rain and
the echoed sounds
of footsteps and perhaps
a soft stolen midnight kiss or two
under the sweet dim lamplight.

Floating On the Vistula

Floating on the Vistula past
Wawel Castle's glorious stone walls,
riverbanks dotted with bikers,
hikers, lovers and sleepers,
stationary on a boat, but
moving slowly all the same,
as if time were taffy and
you were part of the pull,
water glistening with sunlight,
nowhere to go, but nowhere
else you'd rather be than
here, in the quiet moment,
with your family, some pretzels
and a lovely cold coke,
crammed into little chairs
and a tiny table on deck while

the guide at the mike tells you
all you need to know and more,
her voice fading in and out as if a siren
calling out from the top of Wawel Cathedral,
drawing you toward your past and present
(and sometimes in between the shimmering,
simmering cracks),
until you shake loose from the daydream
and track down your children in the gorgeous
party room below, with glowing wood,
soft leather booths, a bar that swivels open
and a young couple holding hands
across the table, laughing quietly and
seeing only themselves in a painted picture
of dappled light, while we tiptoe around them
and explore all the neat nooks and crannies of a
curiously curious child's life.

Nine Holes Near Krakow

Nine holes near Krakow,
laid out in the countryside
like soft pieces of cloth,
far away from the hustle & bustle of
the Rynek Główny,
a quiet gift of barely rustling
grass, trees and sunlight,
filled with no-one but
the sleepy golf-pro and
the talkative young cab driver
who drove you to this
Nirvana-like place
in the little village of Ochmanów,
nine holes of the sweetest
solitude as you trudge from
shot to shot, up steep hills
and down the backsides of

others, following the swoops
and curves like a map of your life,
contemplating each shot
like a poem, or a lover's sigh,
surrounded by gorgeous
farmland, red-tile roofed houses,
and occasional distant puffs of
chimney smoke, you swing
and feel in harmony with
the earth and the birds cawing
"dzień dobry" (good morning)
overhead, while the groundskeeper
mows the fairway grass at a steady
humming pace, you look at
the clouds and the horizon
and think of your family
and wish you could share this
magnificent inner moment
when time stands still
and it's just you and the ball

in a manicured Garden of Eden,
thankful for all you have
and hoping you can pass on
this passion for a sport
and the outdoors to your
sons, so they, too, can
feel the joy of one-ness
in places like this,
where Kings once hunted
and deer roam free, baffled
by the man who smiles
and stares at the ever-lightening sky.

In the Dragon Caves

Down the spiral staircase to
the dragon caves,
down deep into
the earth, the
air cooling with
each step round and
round, small slats of
windows slash bits of light,
but full darkness
surrounds at the bottom
and you crawl out
like insects
following the dim light
past colorful
rock flow fields,
drips and slips
on the multi-puddled floor,
surprised
at the endless

tunnels shooting
in all directions
like a smuggler's paradise
and at the end, a
fire-breathing dragon
named Smok sits in
all his glory, spitting out
flames and proclaiming
his proper place in
Krakow's long history,
shuffing out smoke for
all the picture takers
and their eager, wide-eyed
children, who climb
up and peek out from
behind his huge scaly
arms and legs,
smiling sure and strong
as if they have come and
conquered the rough
slouching fearsome beast.

The Performers

Street performers perch
on stilts high above the
crowds, or gyrate clockwise
on their heads to a finger-snapping
boombox beat, or
even pose silent and still
in old-time costumes,
painted entirely gold,
like statues for hours
at a time, one even
sits up in the air on a magic
carpet, a single hand
atop a wooden stick,
others flip a switch and
sing along with recorded
music in distant corners,
the sounds reverberating

large & loud across the
huge pedestrian zone;
the flower market perks
along, birds and tourists
bedeck the tall poet's statue
and horse-drawn carriages
click-clack by like clockwork,
but the beautifully off-beat
performers
give the main square
its inner electricity, glow &
life, gathering curious crowds
to see who & what they are
on a sweet summer's
day or soft, enchanted
midsummer's night.

Wieliczka

Descending into the Wieliczka Salt Mine
involves step after step after step
(four hundred in all)
down a wooden staircase,
with the air cooling by degrees
on each landing
until you reach bottom
and walk and walk and walk
through long tunnels
into huge chambers filled
with sculptures made
by the miners, plus countless
chapels, chandeliers,
murals, altars, shrines,
all miraculously carved from salt,
even the massive two-story reception hall
big enough to hold a wedding

or a football game,
hewn out of the ground
over eight hundred years,
impressive, gigantic, and yet
full of lonely shadows,
all those men laboring
underground when torches
were used for lights
and salt was more valuable
than gold,
an amazing sight
(there's even a restaurant!)
one that you really wouldn't know
is there until you take a chance
and head down below the earth,
step by
    step by
        steady, patient step.

The Brides of Krakow

Sitting around the Saturday square,
looking out at all the people
passing softly by as if they
were in a silent symphony of
hunger, sight-seeing and thirst,
all hoping to sit and
rest and watch the people
passing by too,
but then a clip-clop of hoofs
is heard, coming closer and
closer until, finally, a sleek
horse-drawn carriage appears
with a smiling bride and groom
inside, happy on their special
day, gorgeous and young,

the billowing white bridal
dress barely fitting inside
the cart, taking a tour of
the cobblestone paths before
the wedding begins, only to be
followed by another bride & groom in
another carriage, and yet another
and another, until it seems as
if everyone is getting married on
this spectacular day in June,
and the lemon flavored iced tea
in hand is cool and refreshing
and the sky is sparkling blue like
a bride's bright knowing eyes.

Lody

Ice cream stands on every corner,
delicious, creamy, soft-serve stuff
that kids & parents & grandparents
love to eat with big happy licks,
curved swirls of delight called lody,
sold everywhere you turn in Krakow
(just like the ubiquitous kebab),
from street vendors, little shops
or through tiny windows,
it soothes the Polish soul,
cool chocolate or vanilla
swishes of sweet joy,
carry it along carefully
under the hot summer sun,
be quick to catch the errant drips,
& watch the scenery & dodge
the occasional aggressive electric
trolley car, cab or horse carriage
rolling noisily by.

In the Engine Room

So many airplane engines
in one single room,
all oiled, polished,
elegant, dynamic,
like modern sculptures,
cool, pristine, commanding,
able to power airplanes
up and away and bring
them back again,
such feats of engineering
skill and craftsmanship,
all alone and proud
in a soaring, curved hangar
at Krakow's Aviation Museum,
does someone dust them
off each week or polish
them up to keep the shine,

do they get many visitors
without the fancy trappings
of plane bodies and wings,
or are these the souls of
the planes, preserved for
all to see, the center of
each plane's universe,
where all the hum and purr
and zip originates to fuel
mankind's flight into the future
and battles with foes in
war after war after war,
who were the courageous
pilots who went up with some
of these earliest engines and
just canvas, wood and wire for
protection, who felt the wind
on their cheeks and the rain
on their goggles and bonded
with the elements until man

and engine and nature were one,
trying to capture what birds have
always known, that flight
is a gift of mystical curve,
aerodynamics, prayer,
muscle, thought and bone,
and endless, restless heart,
which engines can only try to emulate,
roaring in the heavens
for sweet moments aloft before
swift returns to the plodding,
muddy earth below.

Pizza with Ketchup

Pizza with ketchup
right smack dab in
the center,
carefully placed,
round and red,
full of meaning,
taste and fun for
the Polish palate,
but it wasn't what
my son was used to,
so we negotiated with
fumbling Polish/English
words and big hand
gestures for a hamburger
instead at the little
fast food restaurant
just outside the magical,
mystical world of the
magnificently-cool Krakow Zoo.

At The Krakow Zoo

Little children in a row
holding onto a long
padded, multi-colored snake
walk softly single-file
past the animals,
(some of whom look sleepy, as if
deep in a sweet dream of running
swift and free through Krakow's
cobblestoned streets),
keeping together,
safe in large numbers,

a long rainbow of love
that binds them all together
in one beautiful bundle
as the blue peacock struts and
squawks and the zoo
awakens to the sound of
young voices, like
a magician's box,
full of amazing secrets,
that only a child's eyes
can see.

Watching the Birds

Watchin' the birds
up in the sky
swoopin' the loops,
happy as pie,
chasin' the leader
who knows the way,
'round the church tower
where the trumpeter plays,
swingin' down easy,
comin' down soft,
smooth glass landing
near the poet's high loft,
feastin' on bagels
chattin' the breeze
eyein' the procession
of all those big knees.

The Trumpeter in the Tower

The trumpeter in the tower
leans out a small west window
with brass in hand,
puts lips to horn and
blows out his hourly song,
proud as a peacock spreading
its multi-colored feathers full of
history to remind everyone of
an ancient attack on Krakow
by invading forces,
his current soulful tune interrupted
during the final note just like
the first trumpeter almost eight hundred
years ago, hit by a brilliant arrow-shot
before the music could finish,
a wave of the hand and the
trumpeter disappears,

only to show up at three
other windows (east, south,
north) to put the same mournful song
out into the air for all in
the huge square below to
hear.

Thinking of Glasses

Thinking of glasses,
piled high and deep,
all sorts of colors and bends,
twists and curves,
reflecting each other and
the viewer, the light
bending in a dozen
skewered directions,
each pair belonged to someone,
a mother, father, sister, brother,
uncle, cousin, grandparent,
ripped from happy homes
and families and sent to Auschwitz,
brutal camp of nightmares,
crusher of life and dreams,
soul-smasher of the stars,
snuffing out sparks before

they had a chance to change
the world in even the smallest way,
piles of glasses, inert, lifeless,
cracked, spent, defeated,
astonishingly gripping,
full of fear and cries for help,
and nearby, a huge pile of shoes,
another of suitcases,
still another of artificial limbs,
and a small mountain of hair,
horrible evidence of lives snatched away
for reasons still difficult to understand,
by people trying to play God and
change the course of the life,
who were finally washed away and exposed
as demons of intergalactic proportions
no more important than the precious tiny glasses
that once fit a young girl's head and let her see
a once-innocent world clearly as she ran to play
with her friends after school on a sunlit Polish afternoon.

Boys in Big Plastic Bubbles

Boys in big plastic bubbles
blown full of air and
floating on the Park Jordana pond,
sealed into a world of Krakow fun,
rolling, running, slipping,
sliding, laughing like
a lifetime supply of Kraft
Macaroni & Cheese was
suddenly theirs at no charge,
astonished at the energy
needed to push the ball around
with all their might,
bursting with energy
as they toss and tumble
until the time-clock blings
and the man on the dock
shouts in Polish and then
slowly reels the little boy fishes
in by pulling on the attached ropes,
unzips the side bubble zippers
and pulls the pint-sized Jonahs
out and onto dry land,
panting, eyes bright,
all they can say is,
that was so totally cool and
can we please do it again right now.

Shining Stars

Walk into a church
in Krakow on a Sunday and
you'll barely find a seat,
standing room only,
anywhere you look
ornate swirls and
carvings abound
painted with gold and red and blue
but the blue starred sky in
St. Mary's Church
takes
your breath
away
as you crane your
neck to take
in all its interplanetary
shiningness,

reflecting the
reverence Poland has
for its religion
and shrines
and prayer
and God,
which are part of the
fabric of everyday life,
like eating, sleeping,
learning, talking,
with a bit of the stuff
of dreams thrown in
for good measure
Amen.

Magical Medieval McDonald's

In the magical medieval McDonald's,
with all the foods listed in Polish
but all the uniforms and crowds
and excited children the same
as anywhere around the world,
you take your tray and head downstairs
and suddenly, you're no longer in
modern day Krakow, you're
descending instead back through time
a thousand years, as the walls turn
to brick and the vaulted curved ceilings
surround you until you reach the first of
many interconnected ancient rooms
with red brick walls, gorgeous
old ceilings and tiny dungeon-like windows
high up and inaccessible letting in
feeble bits of light,

you wander from room to room astonished
at where you are, disoriented because
you're eating today's hamburger in
a thousand-year-old room where
knights may have once met and
casks of wine or possibly trunks laden
with gold or fine silk cloth may once have
been stashed for safekeeping,
the stone floor adds that final special touch
and you nosh contentedly with your family
knowing that you'll most likely never see
a McDonald's like this anywhere
around the fast-spinning world again.

The Wood Carvings

Rustic stalls full of wooden chess sets,
bowls and beautiful boxes
(with curved designs on each side),
some packed so tight with objects
the seller sits in a little center
area and crawls out through a low
hinged half-door to take a break,
but the wood carved figurines
and panels are the ones that
break your heart with such sad, lined
peasant faces & titanically tired eyes,
almost as if life has been just too much to bear
since time began to grin and growl,
so you search and search for
that elusive carving that has some joy,
some zest, some zing, until,
finally, you see it, back in a stall
alcove, completely hidden from view,

three thick-mustached musicians
in old-time mountain outfits
sitting on wooden benches
by a fireplace, all chiseled in relief
on a simple rectangular piece of wood, with
dashes of color here and there on hats and coats
and a slight polished sheen,
you hold the work in your hands and
stare in disbelief at the glint of soft happiness
captured in a musical moment,
even though the men don't smile,
you can tell that they know each other
and the songs they play well,
their instruments pulled perhaps
from pegs on a wall after a hearty soup
dinner and the weight of impossible
dashed hopes and dreams lifted
for a moment, as if they have escaped
from monotony and flown to the
mountaintops of the purest white snow
or valleys with flowers in full, fragrant summer bloom.

In the Spin

In the Krakow dance-clubs,
down below the ground,
deep in the cellars that
go back a thousand years,
rugged brick walls with
arched passageways and
catacomb-like intrigue,
bars are set up, with couches
and tables in interconnecting
rooms (sometimes you even
have to crawl under a low stone
archway & watch your head),
ultra-cool and full of
spinning silver disco balls of
different sizes almost like
an array of planets and moons,
reflecting colored light
on the floor and dancers' faces

jumpin' and jivin' to the
electric techno DJ beats,
the heat of human sweat
and college-age hormones
hangs heavy in the air, but some
are just there for the fun of it
and the knot of humanity
into which we're all packed,
dancing and toasting our
existence, hailing our own
personal musical gods,
doesn't it all boil down to
shaking out the blues,
twisting and turning,
feeling the pulse,
like a universal heartbeat
of love, pulling men and women
together in the dim light,
allowing them to be free and
unencumbered by their
daily Crakovian cares and woes.

The Black Madonna

People are packed tightly
into the Jasna Góra Monastery church
to get a glimpse of the mystical Black Madonna
painting above the altar,
shoulder to shoulder, chanting,
moving, praying, thinking,
the sounds swelling like
ocean waves during a storm,
filling the space with the
busy hum of humanity and
thought so dense that perhaps
God can't make the messages out,
but he always does,
the mass ends and the silver
cover comes down, protecting
the painting from harm,
dust and light, and the people

disperse back to their cars and lives
moved by this visit to
Częstochowa and this sacred
relic, damaged by conquest and
time, but proud and shining
like a quiet beacon of interior
truth, hope and light,
illuminating lives and
paths that lead over
mountains, hillsides and
waters to small humble
homes and children
saying simple prayers in bed
on cold winter nights.

Krakow Sits Like a King

Krakow sits like a king
in all its old stone glory
cobblestones all aglow
horse carriages clip-clopping
like the ticks of an ancient clock
while people mill and shop
in the massive main square
unaware that the people they're watching
are watching them too
everyone so relaxed in the cafes,
whiling away the time over
wine and Żywiec beer,
catching up on the day,
making small talk,
listening to the sounds
of everyday life, love and song,

pigeons fluttering up and down,
sometimes circling around and
around together as if a signal
or switch has been thrown,
the town is alive with youth,
students, bike riders,
laughter, sighs and the rustle
of shopping bags moving by
long live the king,
brawny, delicate, marvelous
and so sweet,
like Szarlotka, that wondrous
Polish apple cake!

Bubbles On the Pond

Two boys back in big plastic bubbles on a pond
rolling, tossing, turning,
laughing like chocolate comets
were passing by and dropping off
tasty bits to eat,
slippin' & a slidin',
unable to stand up
for more than a few seconds,
moovin' & a groovin'
like outer-space break dancers,
beautiful and free
& wide awake, suddenly
supercharged with
all the gorgeous unlimited
effervescences of life,
forgetting the silly rules
and focusing in on
the sheer atomic power
of Fun.

In the Sukiennice Museum

In the Sukiennice Museum,
quiet as a church,
your sneakers squeak
and the guard gives you
a stern look, but you
can't stop the squeaking
so you just tiptoe by
and look at the beautiful
19th century Polish paintings
and sculptures in
four large rooms with
high ceilings and a grand,
salon-like air,
all reached by a swirling
staircase with a glass and
steel elevator in the center,
you peer at the works

and they're amazing but
you've never heard of the
painters before, yet
they're as good as Monet,
Manet, Renoir and others
of their era and you wonder
why no one knows about them,
it's a real puzzle and then
you get to the huge canvases
depicting rich, colorful scenes
(like Chełmoński's massive "Four-in-Hand"
painting of a carriage with four racing
horses that almost leaps alive into the room),
historic moments & famous Polish battles
won and they take up entire walls,
all stunning in scope and detail,
you need to sit down to absorb
them all, feel their power and
study the stories told,
big pictures hanging on the wall,

hidden histories in each,
brush-strokes of genius,
tucked away in a jewel of a museum
above the Cloth Hall that
you really have to hunt to find,
you take a deep breath and sigh,
glad to make the artists' acquaintance
and happy to know you didn't walk past
and forget to see what's going on inside.

The Wild, Wicked Bus Ride

The wild, wicked bus ride
to Zakopane started out so peacefully,
so serene in the Krakow bus station,
the big bus pulled in slowly and nudged along
to the end of its parking spot and
passengers piled in, but then the drivers
changed and the fun started,
the uniformed woman who grabbed the wheel
was in a hurry (and a fury) of some
tornado-ish sort and she clearly wasn't
going to let cars and pedestrians get in her
speed-demon way,
she came so close to hitting so many cars,
people, and trucks, that it soon became a white-knuckle
rollercoaster ride, but to top things off, she
also spent most of the drive talking on her cell-phone
with one hand while steering with the other,

honking, passing, veering, flooring it as though
the bus was nearing the final flag in the Indianapolis 500
race, but no one dared to go up and tell her to
slow down since she exuded such a fierce warrior queen look,
there were obviously problems at home or with children,
parents or boyfriends, but we got to Zakopane so quickly
we had more of the day than we expected to roam
around before checking into our quaint,
chalet-style hotel with carved wood all around,
so she actually did her job well, just in a
strange, sat-on-a-cactus, kick-boxing title match mad
state that broke through the boundaries on our lives for
a few hours and rattled our collective cages in a
beautifully deranged, frighteningly dangerous,
magnificently Halloween-scare way.

Sizzling Fiddlers Sling

Sizzling fiddlers sling
out notes in Zakopane
from each rustic restaurant
along the main street
basses plunking boldly
to keep the big beat
while the fleet-fingered
accordionists add crisp, crackling
logs to the soaring gypsy bonfire
before the musicians

break out into sudden song
with stout backs and full hearts,
as if pulling a cart loaded
with large musical notes from the
mountains to each shepherd,
each girl in a colorful peasant dress,
each wandering tourist sitting
over wine and beer and peering
for a while into Poland's
festive, foot-stomping soul.

Zakopane By Night

All that amazing meat,
piled high on huge grills in
every Zakopane restaurant,
chicken and beef kebabs,
pig's knuckles, anything
and everything,
sizzling and roasting
over wood-fire flames,
stoked by attentive
grill-meisters adorned
in colorful Tatra Mountain
village shirts with vibrant
stitching around the collars,
thick round wood beams
on the ceilings all around,
and foot-tapping music
thrown up and out like

shouts and claps from
deep within the Polish soul,
walk the streets at night
and inhale the wonderful
meat smells, hear the laughter
and clinks of glass, feel
the warmth of the
snarling, snapping fires,
and dream of hikes & sights
to come tomorrow,
when the sun rises
and the grills are silent
and still, and waiting
for the first flick of
a match to ignite
the magic all over again.

Cable Car to Kasprowy Wierch

Soaring in a cable car,
mountain beauty flashing all around,
valleys, houses, ski-runs,
craggy peaks all appear
in shrouded mist and then vanish,
patterns and paths emerge,
like veins in a Giant's arms,
feel the frightening "bump"
each time the car goes over
a supporting post,
passenger breath fogging
up the windows,
(mist on the outside,

fog on the inside now)
and yet the craggy majesty
of Kasprowy Wierch is too
bold to slip entirely from view,
see the hostel high
on the hill,
impossible to reach,
but somehow, someway,
summer hikers find a route,
like trickles of water
seeking a path that
only the secret universe inside
each sacred drop can know.

Hot Roasted Potatoes

Top of the Tatra Mountains in the rain,
trekking slowly down a stone path
to a nearby peak,
Slovakia on one side,
Poland the other,
we turn back toward the
cable car station and
look out toward distant Zakopane,
far below and surrounded by glowing green,
sun spotlighting bits and pieces
of the countryside through the clouds,
the big bowl at the top of the ski-run area
gaping beneath us,

a spectacular panorama
shared with my sons,
something to tuck deep and remember
as we head back in for a bowl of
red borscht, pizza and some
heavenly heaps of hot roasted potatoes,
with big black/white pictures of
Polish skiing greats up on the walls
looking down on our little
fleeting family feast.

Morskie Oko In The Rain

Sitting side-by-side in a covered
wood wagon while the horses clip-clop
along up the steep road, a
light beige canvas stretched
taut overhead like a tunnel and
lashed down on the sides with rope,
hikers slogging behind in the rain
appearing and receding like people
in a slowly waking dream,
the gentle shake of the wagon lulls
and friendly conversations with
elbow-to-elbow neighbors flow
like beers from secret taps,
clocks seem to have vanished,
held prisoner between the sweet drops of rain
and the sense that you're moving back and forth
in time in the same nit-split second,

shimmering, turning, folding, unfurling,
holding more clues than you have knowledge to use
as the wagon passes more hikers, all seeking a
similar destination, a higher point, a sense of self
and soul at the tip of a long journey's completion,
but the wagon softly turns, circles, and you disembark,
amazed at the steam rising off the horses' haunches,
bathed in the soft rinse from the sky,
ready for the last mile or two trek up to Lake Morskie Oko,
which turns out to be gorgeous, shrouded in fog
and still, as if a shrine to all that is good, clean, fresh
and full of songs as yet unsung.

Barszcz

Barszcz soup,
hot and delectable,
ever-present at each meal,
ten thousand shades of red,
no two the same,
croquettes on the side
(some big, some small),
soft-lit by candlelight,
steam curling up past the
bright bits of flame,
nearby conversations muffle,
clear, then vanish again,
like smuggled communications
in clandestine corner booths,
all speaking the secret language
of hot red beet soup,

sipped slow and sacred,
with just a dash of salt,
the sweet promise of
hot Szarlotka soon to come,
while the fiddlers
fiddle away and people looking
for their own beautiful
bowls of hot barszcz
pass slowly by.

Shooting the Tracks

Rolling up the funicular rail line
to Gubałówka Hill,
a quick bop to the top
to soak in the sweet
panoramic views of green
Tatra Mountains and zesty
Zakopane down below,
suddenly you spot a
shining steel runway
filled with steep curves,
working its way down a bit
of the mountain and little
go-kart like cars speeding
through the convoluted paces,

drawn like metal to a strong magnet
you take the plunge and ride
with your young sons as if
on bareback horses, yelping
to high heaven like the world
was on fire and you're carrying
the last good piece of wood,
at the bottom, a big hook catches
onto your go-kart and pulls you up the
steep slope to the starting line,
you pay your fee, shake and bake
your fast-pumping heart and do it all over
again with a pure, childlike
shout that a tall, bearded Slovakian hiker
with superior ears just pulling himself
up to the highest nearby mountain top
might faintly hear and ponder
aloud at God's wondrous silly plans.

At the 7-D Movies

Sitting in a 7-D movie theater
in early evening Zakopane,
when the gift stalls are half-closed
& people are resting up a bit
before the dinner rush begins,
wondering what it's all about
when the show starts
and the seats move,
winds blow,
big sounds surround,
bits of rain (or is it snow) fall,
and objects float
on and off the screen
in the most peculiar ways,
bombarding our senses
and providing lots of giddy laughs,
surprising us with new thrills in a
silly, offbeat carnival
side-show way.

The Eagle in The Rocks

On a lashed-together wooden raft,
we float,
gently,
softly,
drifting along with the current
as two men in colorful vests
push us along with twelve-foot-long poles,
the rhythm of their dips and pushes
constant and reassuring,
but then the rapids approach
and we pick up speed
as the soaring jagged cliffs
of the Dunajec Gorge appear,
lock-into view and then pass behind,
more natural gems to store away
in the recesses of the travel mind,

now hear a story in Polish, told
by the elder boatsman, who speaks
with the confidence of years on the Dunajec River,
his pride in his craft
bursting through like a bright sun,
someone translates in a whisper
and the joke comes alive, he's
a character, alright, and you're glad
he's running the show because the
younger pole-slinger in the back of the
raft keeps splashing water on you
with each long surging stroke,
the raft seems to be as ancient as the hills,
with visible nail, metal and tar repairs
and yet you trust its magic as you
slip back and forth across the Poland/
Slovakian border in the singing river,
with hikers waving, laundry flapping
in backyards, cliff-climbers perched

high above and a cool eagle pattern in
the rocks and, most of all, Fat Chris,
the marvelous, talkative taxi driver
who drove you from Zakopane
to the river dock, is there,
just as he promised,
waiting for you in the next town at the end
of the ride, as if in a dream created by the
lulling, sultry song of the curving,
endless, deep-green Polish countryside.

Sitting in a Swing

Sitting in a swing in a
hard-to-find Zakopane pub,
right up against the square-shaped,
round-edged bar counter that frames
the sturdy, droll, bearded bartender
cleaning the glassware and pouring
the soothing sips,
four backyard swings made of
rope, leather and wood,
hang from the ceiling,
letting you spin and swirl and drift
in your own thoughts while
the locals spotting in on the stools

speak soft Polish (including the neighborhood
postman who's just finished his
rounds and placed his worn leather mailbag
on a nearby empty chair, happy to slip-off and
shed his sorting & delivering burdens of the day,
but he has the glorious gift of wit and
makes the other locals laugh from time to
time with ease), conversations flit
back and forth like butterflies and more
people trickle in as darkness deepens through
the tinted windows and this hidden island of smooth
shaped wood, curved clear bottles full of multi-hued
liquids, and easy-pulling beer taps closes in
and binds all of these willing and unwilling participants
together for a few minutes in a little rustic town
at the base of the magnificent Tatra Mountains,
so full of outdoor swagger and sprawling soaring
gorgeous green.

The Doors

Tall double doors loom on every block,
massive, thick, strong, foreboding,
towering overhead like NBA centers
blocking shots at the hoop,
glaring fiercely at all who pass by,
growling at small dogs and children,
full of deep, dark, dreamy elegant colors,
reds, greens, browns, blues,
some with small doors cut into larger ones,
for quick and easy entry without opening
the huge multi-hinged goliaths (but only
for renters, owners and janitors with a secret skeleton
key), once inside these gorgeous old buildings,
the vestibules gleam with worn marble
stairs and walls and wrought-iron railings

that curve in intricate waves and patterns that
only creative, experienced welders and artists
can shape, each landing full of well-used areas that
tell stories of people past and present,
where children ran past drumming fingers again and
again on the wall and old-timers with canes paused to
scold or catch a needed breath or look out a window into
the courtyard to see young lovers leaning into each
other's arms in endless embrace, never to let one another
go, while a middle-aged mother hangs dripping laundry
on the clothesline and a distant dog barks, chasing
bits of sunlight filtering through the gently waving green
summer tree leaves and dancing nimbly on the hard
brown dirt and scattered simple shards of struggling grass.

Walking Around the Planty

Walking around the Planty,
Krakow's wide green ring of
gorgeous grass, trees and cafes,
relaxing on a bridge made
of curved wrought-iron
& gazing out over the pond
as the fountains shoot up
in the air from time to time,
snapping pictures here and there
because you're bummeling along,
looking at life slowly, putting
the clocks away for a moment,

touching the century-old bricks
of the city walls and listening
to the colorfully dressed
trumpeter and accordionist
play their catchy folksongs
for passersby, a little old Babcia,
hands gnarled with age sitting
just behind on a bench,
eating lunch and throwing
scraps of bread to the birds,
who flock to her black-shoed feet.

Last Night

Last night in paradise,
eating roasted chicken
in a little out of the way place
with colorful wood-carvings of
clucking hens and roosters
above the entrance door and
simple wooden tables with checked
red and white tablecloths,
self-serve at the ordering window
with the chef peeking out from time
to time to slide a completed order
through the slot,
clean white light shining on all the walls
as if you've been bathed in sacred waters
and purified, soothed, whispered-to and
patted on the back, massaged in
multitudinous magnificent ways
and made whole, fresh and new,

ready to be packaged up and mailed back
home from Poland like a shiny brand new car just about
to be driven off the showroom floor,
each knob gleaming, each piece of upholstery
untouched, a masterwork of craftsmanship
fully prepared to explore the world,
a brand new soul,
renewed, forgiven, enlivened, re-charged,
knowing once more who you were and would
like to be,
unique,
undulating,
percolating,
perfect,
a traveler ready to go home,
where the same world is different
and the different world the same,
alive, alert, amazed, awake,
searching only for the comfort
now of your old pillow, sheets, bed and books.

Joseph Kuhn Carey is the recipient of an American Society of Composers, Authors and Publishers (ASCAP)/Deems Taylor Award for music-related writing (for articles written about jazz artist/composers Carla Bley, Charlie Haden and Anthony Braxton) and a Grammy-voting member of The Recording Academy. He's published a chapbook of poetry ("Bulk-Rate") and a book on jazz ("Big Noise From Notre Dame: A History of The Collegiate Jazz Festival," University of Notre Dame Press) and has released two "Loose Caboose Band" CDs of original children's songs with his brother, Bill, entitled "The Caboose is Loose" and "Mighty Big Broom," the latter of which garnered two first-round Grammy nominations in 2008 (both recordings, and all of the individual songs, are available on iTunes, CDbaby.com and Amazon.com). He received a Bachelor of Arts degree in English from the University of Notre Dame, a Master of Fine Arts (in Creative Writing) degree from the University of Iowa Writers' Workshop and a Master of Science in Mass Communication degree from Boston University. He's traveled the country interviewing bakers for Bakery Magazine, written about jazz & blues artists for Down Beat, JazzTimes and The Boston Globe, and his poems have been selected in the Journal of Modern Poetry's JOMP 15 and JOMP 16 Poetry Contests, the Writer's Digest 7th Annual Poetry Awards Contest & 80th Annual Writing Competition, Highland Park Poetry's 2013 "Poetry That Moves" & 2013 "Poetry Challenge" contests and the Evanston Public Library's 2013 35th Annual Jo-Anne Hirschfield Memorial Poetry Awards. When not scribbling poems, stories and songs on all available scraps of paper to read to his wife and sons over dinner, he runs a successful multi-state property management business.

Additional copies of this book can be ordered through
PostcardsfromPoland.com